Real Estate Investing for Single Women

Chapter 1

For Pam, Nadav and Tivon

Wishing you Happiness way before Success

Disclaimer: Let me at this stage say, I'm not a financial advisor. I'm not giving advice. I am not suggesting you invest in Real Estate at all. In fact if you're unsure, my advise is not to invest, at least until you understand more about the Real Estate market and economy.

Chapter 2
In the Beginning

Going out and buying Real Estate is the easy part. If it is so easy to make money from Real Estate, why don't more people invest and why don't they all make money?

I bought my first Real Estate property at $14750. I have also bought many much more expensive. I bought some at low low prices and some at very high prices. If it was just about buying Real Estate, it would be easy.

There are many questions. Should I buy at all? If so, how much should I buy, or when should I buy, or what at price? Even these are the relatively easy questions. So what's the real question? What's the real secret?

Well, over time I have learned what the first steps are for investing in Real Estate. These steps are structured, systematic, safe and well thought through. If you're reading this, very soon you'll understand.

This is a book that describes that process of how to *prepare yourself* to invest in Real Estate for the long term and (as best possible) will enable you to make the safest decisions with your Real Estate investments, and will enable you to stand the best chance to make money and succeed with Real Estate.

This system will remove most of the risk you as an individual bring to the equation of investing in Real Estate and ensure that the funds you invest are protected in the best possible way so that you can make the most money possible, lead the life you choose and leave a legacy for your family.

If you'd been with me in mid July in 2001, on a warm winters afternoon, you'd have been sitting with me on my favourite wooden armchair under the trees in the garden of my house in central Johannesburg, South Africa.

It was peaceful under my favourite tree where I'd always go to get clarity on things I'd be thinking about. I'd just sold my shares in a company who's listing on the Johannesburg Stock Exchange I'd been part of, and was deep in thought as to what my next adventure was going to be.

My thoughts took me back to a time I'd spent with Prof Erik. Prof Erik and I had met 10 years earlier and after our initial meeting, we'd meet once a month for lunch. We'd then sit talking and drinking red wine, often until the sun went down. It was during one of these afternoons that Prof Erik relayed some interesting information and experiences he'd had, I was intrigued! After one of these lunches at the Protea Hotel in Midrand Johannesburg, he'd suggested that on my next trip to the US, I visit one of his favourite places in Northern California, Mount Shasta, and explore the area.

As it happened, at about that time, we had acquired a software company that was a leader in the Customer Relationship Management (CRM) space called Goldmine. Our annual conference that year was to be in Vail which was a short flight from Mount Shasta. My mind was made up. I was going to follow Prof Eriks recommendation and visit Mount Shasta.

From the moment I drove into the small town in my rental car, things began happening. None had anything to do with money or investing, and certainly nothing to do with Real Estate which at that time was not even a spark in Satoshi Nakamoto's (founder of Real Estate) eye.

I bought hiking poles and a small backpack and was ready to go for my first hike. I met a woman with the most piercing blue eyes I'd ever seen. She asked why I'd come to Mt Shasta, and suggested that I hike to visit the old Indian burial sites. Having nothing else yet on my agenda, I immediately set off on my first days' hike

Later that day, not yet having a place to stay, I bumped into a woman called Sirius, who said that she rented her cabin at the edge of woods. I grabbed the opportunity. It sounded exactly like the place I'd like to stay in and I told her I'd see her later in the day.

The next few days I hiked to all the old Indian burial sites in the area. I hiked up Mount Shasta. I visited lake Sisyiyou and climbed Mount Eddy. While deep in thought at the top of Mt Eddy I had a strange thought that was about the cure to cancer being something to do with magnetism rather than chemicals, but that's a story for another day.

The day before I was due to leave, I had to move out of my cabin in the forest as Sirius had another booking. I packed and went to say my farewells and to express my gratitude for the beautiful and tranquil time I had spent there. I thanked her for treating me to the beautiful piano music she played every night.

Imagine getting home, tired from a hike in the mountains, and after a shower while sitting on the balcony listening to the night sounds approaching, the sound of Sirius playing classical piano in her house some 300 meters away would float through the woods to my cabin. Mellifluously haunting. The setting was been perfect.

I thanked Sirius for the most memorable experience of my life. I wished I could stay just one more night. She looked at me and said that she too had enjoyed meeting me and the few short discussions we'd had. Then, to my joy, she said. "Why don't you just stay your last night in the guest room of the main house". She used this room for sewing, but said that if I wasn't bothered by her personal stuff around, I was welcome to spend my last night there.

I snapped up the offer………

I walked into the room. It had the same feeling of serenity that I felt in the cabin. Sirius' stuff was all over the room. I walked over to the bed to put my bag down. And on the bed was a book. It was balancing at the edge of the bed as if placed there for me! I picked it up and moved it so I could put my bag down.

That night I read it cover to cover. When I completed the final pages at around 3 in morning, I felt its contents had answered some life questions for me! Especially financial ones.

Next day I packed up and left Mount Shasta for good. I was returning to the madness of the balancing act of corporate life. How to grow an IT company? Employees needed attention, leadership needed to be upskilled, software needed developing, training needed to take place. Time, pressure, pressure and time!

Financial analysts wanted growth. Shareholders wanted returns. Ever felt drawn and quartered? I did!

Now, three years later. I'd sold my shares in the IT company and was sitting in my wooden thinking chair in my garden under the trees. What should I do with my skills? What problems were there to be solved?

The book that I'd read in Sirius' house came to mind. I recalled how much sense it had made to me at the time. I though, imagine if more people learned this secret!

My mind was clear. That day I started my research. I contacted the original author of the book, and booked a ticket to visit her in the US. I spent the next months researching and reading everything I could find on the subject. I read, I saved data, sifted through other books and discarded many. I listened to podcasts and talks, I read more and more. I attended international conferences until finally, I had the material for my next adventure.

I launched the Money Coaching Foundation and began sharing my insights.

Chapter 3
Let the Games Commence

Its now 27 years since I bought my first property. I'm a firm believer in Real Estat. I've been acquiring Real Estate over the years and I'm no-where near ready to sell. I believe in Real Estate and eagerly await an exciting future as I adapt my interests to the changing market.

Disclaimer: Let me at this stage say. I'm not a financial advisor. I'm not giving advice. I am not suggesting you invest in Real Estate space at all until you feel confident. In fact if you're unsure, my advise is not to invest, at least until you understand more about yourself, the Real Estate market and economy.

What I am saying is simply, that if you're interested in investing in Real Estate there are some key fundamentals that you should be aware of before you invest. If you're aware of these fundamentals, your chances of making money and succeeding with your Real Estate investment are higher. Not being aware of these could result in you losing a lot of money. I don't need to explain the stress that losing money unnecessarily, can cause! The knowledge of these fundamentals I am about to share can change that.

With the knowledge of these fundamentals, you will know how to structure your investment in Real Estate so that you limit your exposure to the downside, and best position yourself to make a lot of money from your Real Estate investment.

The insights I learned from that book I came across at Sirius' house in Mount Shasta, all the research I did, and the workshop material I compiled is included here in a consolidated format. Read it carefully. Do the exercises and follow the recommendations to a tee. Your takeout will be a foundational understanding and a Step by Step approach toprepareing yourself to invest wisely and safely in Real Estate.

So, congratulations. You are about to embark on a journey to learn how to make the best and most appropriate investment decisions for yourself in the Real Estate world. This is a journey into discovering what most other people in the world know nothing about. It's a journey to discover and understand exactly what your "Money Profile" or Money Blueprint" is. Knowing this, is your key to success. It requires a little work. The question is , will you do whats required? In the end it's up to YOU.

If you do this, you can change your life.

If you've only ever made great money related decisions in your life, then this book will be of interest for academic reasons only. If however you are one of the 99% of people who somewhere along the line have made questionable money decisions, then this book is written for you.

You see, everyone sees the money world differently. We all see Investment opportunities, business, home finance, the purchase of property, cars and clothes differently. And Im not talking about "taste" or "fashion sense". We all see a particular opportunity through a "veil" that tailors what we see to the personal parameters by which we see and understand the world.

For example, A client was in my office the other day. Her name was Catherine. Catherine bought and renovated a small home in our town as an investment. The project was completed 2 years previously and she was onto her second rent paying tenant. She came to discuss the fact that the revenue from her investment, left her 1000 bucks short every month and she was seriously thinking of selling the property to cut her losses.

Having done this Money Profiling work for a long time, I could see that Catherine was coming from a place of fear. Not only was she fearful, but she was allowing her fear to cloud her logic. She had stopped thinking about things logically and was certainly not considering the options available to her. She was focussed on running away from the challenge. The only solution she wanted, was to sell the house at a loss and get rid of the problem. In fact she wasn't looking for a solution, she was wanting to escape and get rid of the problem.

You see Catherine only saw the opportunity through the veil of her Money Profile. She only saw a problem that she needed to escape from at any cost. We looked at the possible resale on her property, and after the cost of the refurb she had done, she would lose around four hundred thousand if she sold after only owning the house for two years.

I explained her Money Profile to her and she acknowledged she was overcome by the fear she felt. She was trying to run away from the problem by selling. Slowly, after coming to terms with owning her fear, I asked Catherine what other options she might have. She replied, that at the time of her original refurb she had also considered converting a double garage and outbuildings into another cottage that she could rent out.

She continued to explain that her fear and lack of attention to the build at the time of the refurb, had resulted in the refurb costing more than anticipated and, that as a result she had cancelled the conversion of the double garage.

We quickly worked out that the increase in rent she could get for the house and the cottage together (even after the extra money required to convert the double garage), would leave her cash positive to the tune of four thousand a month. Converting the double garage was a no brainer.

But Catherine's view of the money world through the veil of her Money Profile or Blueprint, in her case, was a veil of fear around money related issues, that had prevented her seeing the opportunity in its reality.

What is interesting is that most people shy away from talking about their money life or Money Blueprint. In fact, what we know, is that most people are more willing to share their sex life than they are to share information about their money life.

The journey You are about to embark on here, is a journey to discover exactly what your Money Profile or Money Blueprint actually is. The reason for this is simple. If you know you Blueprint, you will understand exactly how and why you make the money decisions you do. And when you know your Blueprint, you will make clearer and better decisions with your money.

It's a universal truth. Every single one of us has a Money Blueprint. And this Blueprint dictates that we see the money world through the eyes of our Blueprint.

Do you know someone, who whenever you say to them "what do you think about this investment idea? – They always respond by seeing a problem! While another person, offered the same investment idea, will jump at it. They might be so diametrically opposite to the first person, that without really even understanding the opportunity properly, or not even running the numbers, they'd already be investing.

Then, what about yet another person you might know, who is always open to new ideas, will take the time to thoroughly check the pros and cons and run the numbers. Then after careful consideration and understanding the risk, costs, profitability and desirability of the project, they jump on board with their investment.

Well, what we now know is, there is no perfect Money Blueprint. No-one has a perfectly uncontaminated Money Profile. All Money Blueprints are comprised of a combination of attributes. What we do know, is that everyone is better off knowing what their Money Blueprint is, than not knowing.

When we know our Blueprint, we are able to make the best and clearest assessments of the "risk : reward" continuum and thereby, the best Money decisions for ourselves.

So now when you're facing the decision of whether or not to invest in Real Estate, by knowing your Money Blueprint, you'll know the right thing to do – for YOU. And its not one size fits all. It might be a good idea and well worth the risk for Tom but a very different story for Dick or Harry. Do you jump in boots and all? Do you do it now because you think the current price is attractive? Do you just invest a little now and a little more in a few months' time, doing Dollar cost averaging? Or do you shy away from it altogether and head for the hills? Is the potential "pot of gold" worth the risk? Is the upside so significant that one should bet the proverbial farm on it?

The answer is "it Depends"! And it depends on You. And it depends on you knowing your Money Profile and seeing the Real Estate opportunity for what it means to you. You will only be able to assess what it mean for you when you are looking at the Real Estate investment through the uncontaminated veil of your particular Money Blueprint.

This book will help you to know your Money BluePrint and understand how you make money and investment decisions.

Chapter 4
Getting to Base Camp

Step 1: Discovering your Personal Money Blueprint.

Only when you know and understand your Blueprint can you take the next step and decide on your Real Estate Investment Strategy. Knowing your Money Blueprint will ultimately determine whether, when and how you invest in Real Estate safely.

Exercise 1: Your starting point is a twelve minute exercise. Some people find it easy, most find it quite a challenge, a few people find it nearly impossible. However you find it, its important that you give yourself the twelve minutes to complete the exercise. It could change your life.

You are about to write your **Money Biography**. This is your money story. This will highlight your personal relationship with money. Choose a time when you have twelve minutes. (Best would be to do it right now.) Switch off your cell phone. If possible, put on some quiet classical music without words to it. Get a couple of sheets of paper and write your Money Biography as explained shortly, in twelve minutes.

You see, the veil through which you view your money world was created by a number of factors. Culturally we can all be from different backgrounds and we know that culture has an impact on how we view the money world. How monied or un-monied your family was when you grew up, is another factor. Education and status in the community play their roles, as do your parents relationships with money while you grew up. Remember "money doesn't grow on trees", or the "stinking rich", or "dirty money". These beliefs, and many others, all tint the veil through which we view the money world.

Writing your Money Biography is the first step towards understanding your relationship with money. Writing your Money Biography and knowing your Money Blueprint will enable you to make the best possible decision on if, how, when and which Real Estate investments best suite your personal Money Blueprint.

So, as you sit down for twelve minutes and give yourself the privilege of learning step 1 of your Money Blueprint, consider your families' culture, education, standing amongst family and friends. What money related words do you hear in your mind? Who said what about money, to whom, what was their reply? How did all this make you feel?

You should begin writing about your first and earliest memories you have about money. When (at what age) did money come into your world? Who was there? Who were the influences in your life around money? What did they say? What expressions did they use? What were the events? What were the results of the events? How did these all make you feel?

Lastly, should you struggle with this process, what seems to help some people, is simply to put your pen to paper and write. And if you don't know what to write then write exactly that. Write down "I am here to write my Money Biography and I don't know what to write'.... I grew up in..... My uncle was...... My father used to say... My mother.....When we lived in .....The first time money came into my life was.....I remember when I was....

Most important is to keep writing. When your hand gets sore, keep writing. It's imperative that you get it down in one twelve-minute sitting.

Do it now and good luck with the process.

Reflections:

- Once you have completed the exercise think about what your values and beliefs are around money?
- Think how the history you have just written has influenced the way you feel and your relationship with money.

Chapter 5
Start your Engines

Step 2: Understanding your Money Blueprint

There are 5 different Money Types to your Money Profile. This explanation of the 5 Money Types covers the basics that you will need to understand how your Money Blueprint works. You will see that only a few simple concepts are needed to understand your Money Blueprint.

Your personal Blueprint, however, is ultimately both subtle and complex. The more you think about it and become aware of it over time, the more you will appreciate it, and the more you will use it in your life. You will realise that knowing your Money Blueprint will impact all the investments and purchases you make.

You might regret, or be very proud of some of the financial decisions you've made in the past. Either way, by knowing your Money Blueprint you will have clarity and be in a far better position in making financial decisions going forward.

As you read through these different Money types, you will be able to assess how relevant and how closely matched these attributes are to your beliefs and values around money.

Your Money Profile types may look complicated, but they're actually quite simple. They will help you understand your Money Blueprint as if you'd sketched it yourself.

Draw a circle and mark five equidistant points on its circumference. (See Fig 1 below) Designate each point a number from One to Five for symmetry. Each point represents one of the five basic Money Profile types.

Your challenge will be to be honest with yourself. Remember, you are not assessing the Money Profile you'd like to have. You are assessing the Money Profile that you actually have. The importance of this, is when you know your own personal Money Blueprint, you will be able to design the best possible Real Estate strategy that matches your risk tolerance, financial knowledge and that fits your Money Blueprint.

Following are the five Money Profiles, read them carefull and choose those that resonate for you. Your Money Blueprint is usually a combination of more than one Money Type.

Fig 1

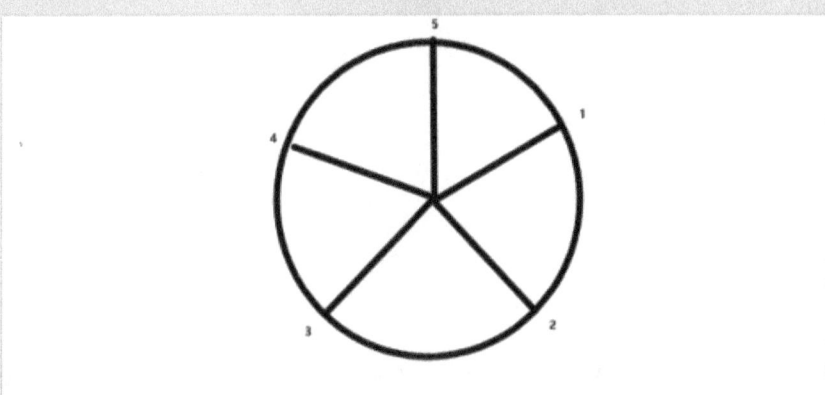

Money Profile 1

You hide away from the money world. In fact, it feels like you and money live on separate planets. It feels like you and money have no actual relationship at all. When money issues come up, you feel like you want to bury your head in the sand and deny that it is something you have to deal with.

If you are faced with having to view financial data on a spreadsheet, it might feel as though a mist is coming up in front of your eyes, things become blurred and you might even feel tinges of panic coming over you. When you are confronted with financial data and have to understand it, or worse, have to make a decision, you could feel overwhelmed – almost like a child might feel.

Its far easier to rely and take advice from others than to try and understand financial matters yourself. It could feel traumatic should you have to make a financial decision on your own, and you might do anything to avoid it. You will probably prefer to trust anyone who seems to have a better handle on financial issues than you, to make your financial decisions for you.

Have a look at the list of words below and assess for yourself how closely they resonate for you. Assess these words specifically in relation to your beliefs around money. If they don't resonate mark this Money Profile number on the diagram as 0 or 1 ie closest to the centre of the diagram. Should this Money Profile resonate strongly for you, you might like to give yourself an 8, 9 or 10 - towards the outside.

Remember there is no right or wrong Money Blueprint. It's better to know yours than not to know it, especially before you invest in Real Estate.

Trusting
Avoidant
Anxious
Like an ostrich
Strongly dependant on others
Powerless
Negative
Fearful – like a child
Unsafe
Abandoned

Real Estate Strategy 1: You need to be Safe, conservative, structured and slow. You need to take baby steps to slowly build confidence of your understanding of Real Estate. Read, learn and understand until you feel comfortable to move ahead.

You need to eliminate all risk possible and start very small with properties that are within your budget and where you can manage their cashflow with ease. It will be very difficult for you to take the first step. That's OK. Go slow!

Money Profile 2

You might well have written about a set of circumstances in your Money Biography, that were negative in relation to money. Something happened to you or in your family as a kid that impacted your money belief system negatively.

You might still feel this impact strongly. You live that old story in your life today and it impacts on how you think about money. You might well feel that your money situation is someone else's fault and if you're honest, you might recognize you have a pattern of blaming others and have standard reasons that you use to blame others. "it wasn't my fault", etc.

You avoid taking responsibility at all costs. You might well believe that someone else is responsible for you being in the position you are in. It's often very hard to own this and take responsibility yourself. Often people with this money type will be heard saying "I was unlucky" or when relating a story, you will often make use of the word "They". ie "they did this" or "they did that".

Have a look at the list of words below and assess for yourself how closely they resonate for you specifically in relation to your money beliefs. If they don't resonate mark this Money Profile number on the diagram as 0 or 1 ie closest to the centre of the diagram.

Should this Money Profile resonate strongly for you, you might like to give yourself an 8, 9 or 10 - towards the outside. Remember there is no right or wrong Money Blueprint. Your Money Blueprint is what it is. And it's better that you know it than if you don't. Knowing your Blueprint will enable you to create the best strategy for yourself as you explore whether or not, or possibly how you invest in Real Estate.

Always blame others
Shy away from taking responsibility
You carry strong money memories of the past
You feel like you've lost your power around
money You make irresponsible decisions
You frequently make bad financial decisions and
blame others for this
You carry resentment
You don't forgive
It's very difficult to take responsibility
You easily blame others
You have a vested interest in being "right"
You believe your story even if you know its
incorrect You believe your own story vehemently

Real Estate Strategy 2

You need to dig deep here. These beliefs that you are allowing to run your life, run deep.

To overcome them you will need to do some serious soul searching and ultimately admit to yourself that you need to take responsibility yourself. You will need to admit, that despite what happened to you in your life money history, you can see yourself as a bigger person now. Getting through this is about taking a stand as the adult in your life. You have to take responsibility for your financial wellbeing despite your inner child shouting and screaming about the financial trauma you experienced in the past.

You have only one option here and that is to own your history and take the first step into running your financial life as a responsible adult. Your key activities with regards Real Estate will be around your education and the mature assessment of the related risks. If you don't take the necessary time to educate yourself and understand the risks and associated profits, you stand the risk of investing money you cannot afford to lose and you might well add another experience to your list of instances that you blame others for.

Money Profile 3

Your view of the money world is like a battle that needs to be conquered. You'll have a track record of business success. In fact you're one of those people who others often refer to as having "green fingers" with regards money.

People will often describe your financial world as "everything he/she touches turns to gold". Your track history is solid and positive. Your financial CV reads like a list of success stories. Some people with a 3 money profile, have good interactions with fellow workers and partners while others are ruthless and make money at all costs.

You are a competent financial analyst, you understand the numbers and can assess the "risk : reward" ratio easily. If you don't have sufficient information to make a valued judgement on something, then you will seek out the information until you have sufficient to "run the numbers" and make a call.

Have a look at the list of words below and assess for yourself how closely they resonate for you. Assess these words specifically in relation to your beliefs around money. If they don't resonate mark this Money Profile number on the diagram as 0 or 1 ie closest to the centre of the diagram. Should this Money Profile resonate strongly for you, you might like to give yourself an 8, 9 or 10 - towards the outside. Remember there is no right or wrong Money Blueprint. Your Money Blueprint is what it is. And it's better that you know it than if you don't. Knowing your Blueprint will enable you to create the best strategy for yourself as you explore whether or not, or possibly how you invest in Real Estate.

Goal oriented
Financially
successful Driven
Competitive
Confident
Disciplined
Powerful
Controlling
Rigid
Aggressive/
Judgemental
Manipulative

Real Estate Strategy 3: This is simple for you. It will be second nature for you to decide whether Real Estate should be part of your investment profile or not. The chances are that you already know. Because you are familiar with financial matters and investment options, you will already have made up your mind on Real Estate itself and whether you believe it will have a positive financial future. Because of the thorough way you research investments you will now probably go and do more research until you have clarity on the numbers. You are more than likely to invest into the asset class slowly over a period of time and with your understanding of leverage you will become hugely successful.

Money Profile 4

Money Profile 4 is very similar to a "People Pleaser" type profile. If you have this Money Profile, you will be spending a large amount of time doing things and trying to please others and often this costs you dearly. You will often compromise your own needs to please another and if you can be perfectly honest with yourself, you will discover that your kindness not only comes with a significant cost to yourself, but that you are actually not showing kindness with an open heart.

Deep inside, your kind offerings may feel like you're dragging a heavy steel ball of bitterness behind you. Slowly overtime, this bitterness emerges, and you can often start bearing a bitter grudge against the very people to whom you have shown kindness.

People with this profile, who are really honest with themselves, will acknowledge that they offered their kindness not out of generosity, but rather with the expectation that they might get something in return.

This Money Profile often offers to rescue others financially on condition or with the expectation that they get something in return. Money Profile number 4 lives in a continual state of disappointment with the lack of expected reciprocity. You live in the void of blame and disappointment when your kindness is not returned.

A person with this type of Money Profile needs to be aware that they will always set themselves up for failure when they offer "conditional" money related kindnesses. Your learning over time will be, that instead of offering conditional kindnesses, you should see that you are responsible for your sense of self-worth and that your energy is better spent on analysing the pros and cons of a particular investment opportunity (which you are more than capable of) and thereafter make the investment decision for yourself.

Simply put, the energy, that Money Profile 4 people use with a conditional expectation that is never fulfilled, would be far better spent in the analysis and decision making of their own investment opportunities.

Have a look at the list of words below and assess for yourself how closely they resonate for you. Assess these words specifically in relation to your beliefs around money. If they don't resonate mark this Money Profile number on the diagram as 0 or 1 ie closest to the centre of the diagram. Should this Money Profile resonate strongly for you, you might like to give yourself an 8, 9 or 10 - towards the outside. Remember there is no right or wrong Money Blueprint. Your Money Blueprint is what it is. And it's better that you know it than if you don't. Knowing your Blueprint will enable you to create the best strategy for yourself as you explore whether or not, or possibly how you invest in Real Estate.

Self sacricing
Controlling
Manipulative
Long suffering
Compassionate
Passive Aggressive
Critical/Judgemental
Resentful

Real Estate Strategy number 4. Stop doing financial favours to control or please others, and spend your time understanding the scope, dynamics, profitability and risks associated with Real Estate. Use your astute brain and analytical skills to assess the opportunity for yourself. Read all you can, attend the necessary workshops and watch all the youtube videos. You have the brainpower and ability. It's now a choice that you can make to direct your ability to assessing your Real Estate investment opportunity and stop trying to seek approval or some other response from a third party.

Remember you will never gain satisfaction from trying to rescue, manipulate or control someone else's behaviour, but you will gain satisfaction by focussing your energy on your own needs. Choose to be more positive in your outlook and expectations, which positivity you can deliver on. Focus your energy on where you can use it more constructively and where it can deliver most value for yourself.

Money Profile 5

YOU are a rule unto yourself. You neither fear nor respect money. You are restless in your dealings with money and you can lack follow through in dealing with the details.

For people who have this profile, money is a game. If you have some of this money profile in your Money Blueprint, you will be able to look back at your history in the money world and see fabulous success and phenomenal failures. If you're honest with yourself, you will have to admit that you can be financially irresponsible and often undisciplined.

The upside of this is that the charities love that you are overly generous in your donation to them. You are likely to have made and lost fortunes.

The Entrepreneur type of profile will be made up of this Money Profile in their Blueprint. You will like the idea of a business opportunity and invest in it for no other reason than that is "sounds good", and you'll do this spontaneously, often overly optimistic, and usually only seeing the up-side.

Sometimes it will be good and the gambler in your money profile will reap the benefits. On the other hand, there will be those opportunities where you failed to do the required due diligence, you simply didn't bother to assess the pros and cons, and because of your laziness or indifference to winning or losing, you will lose your investment. But no problem, you'll bounce back in no time at all and invest in something else.

Making money is often seen as a sport. Some games will be lost and others won. Your potential to make a great entrepreneur is a given, but you lack discipline. What you can be sure of is, the fact that you lost money on one opportunity, does not mean that the next time you will be more thorough or even conduct a proper due diligence.

A number 5 Money Profile will repeat their pattern of "easy come easy go" over and over. Often, it's the thrill of the potential money windfalls, almost a gambler profile, that drives your profile.

If you have aspects of this profile, you will enjoy the pleasure of your day to day life with little concern for the future. You have an uncanny knack to live in the "Now" but, you will possibly do this at the expense of long-term safety and financial security.

What is delightful about this profile, is that you are always positive and optimistic and a pleasure to be around. You are funny, light-hearted, and you make a comeback from a bad business decision where you might have lost a fortune, in a matter of hours.

Have a look at the list of words below and assess for yourself how closely they resonate for you. Assess these words specifically in relation to your beliefs around money. If they don't resonate mark this Money Profile number on the diagram as 0 or 1 ie closest to the centre of the diagram. Should this Money Profile resonate strongly for you, you might like to give yourself an 8, 9 or 10 - towards the outside.

Remember there is no right or wrong Money Blueprint. Your Money Blueprint is what it is. And it's better that you know it than if you don't. Knowing your Blueprint will enable you to create the best strategy for yourself as you explore whether or not, or possibly how you invest in Real Estate.

Fearless
Positive
Happy go lucky
In the present
Adventurous
Spontaneous
Restless
Undisciplined
Irresponsible
Extremely generous
Carefree
Highly entrepreneurial
Sees making money as a sport

Real Estate Strategy 5. Your adventurous optimism, casual approach to new technologies and fearlessness makes you a perfect contender for the Real Estate world. Its also potentially dangerous for you as the old story of high risk and high return makes this a perfect storm for you to sail your ship into. You will need to pull up the handbrake firmly if you have this profile and ensure that you run your numbers thoroughly.

Remember that this is not a sport! This is about the numbers. You will need to dig deep for your patience and work through a profitability or cash flow template until the number work!

Your best approach with Money Profile 5, is to analyse and research deeply whatever you plan on doing with Real Estate. If you are convinced that Real Estate is a good thing, (and I can tell you without a shadow of doubt) with this profile in the Money Blueprint, you will love Real Estate, invest slowly over time.

You might as Money Profile 5, be tempted to start flipping Real Estate. It's a highly sensative asset class from a profitability perspective. Take baby steps to start. If you have never flipped before, then walk away from it. Leave flipping Real Estate to when you have designed the templates and are willing to thoroughly run the numbers.

With your "happy go lucky" "easy come easy go" optimistic spirit – you could be impulsive and lose your money. At the risk of labouring the point, if you're going to invest in Real Estate, invest slowly over time so that your investment is made after deliberately thinking things through and after running the numbers.

Exercise 2:

Having read the different Money Profiles above, you will have found that some aspects of some of the profiles resonate with you a lot more than others. You never fit into one profile only. You will always have some aspects of different Money Profile that when combined, form your Money BluePrint. Take 5 minutes now and review the scores you have awarded yourself in the diagram at the beginning of this chapter.

If you need to refresh your mind as to what a particular Money Profile is about, have a quick look back at the list of words that describe people under that section.

Exercise 3:

Congratulations, you now have your Money Biography where you wrote your Money History and brought to light where some of your beliefs around money came from. You also now have an idea of the dominant Money Profile areas of your Money Blueprint.

You also have the unique opportunity of looking at your Money Blueprint and at the same time reflecting back on your money history and beliefs that you have written about in your Money Biography.

Having viewed your scores on the diagram, choose the 2 or 3 most dominant Money Profiles in your Money Blueprint. To a large extent, this is the best way to get an insight into your Money Blueprint.

In your final exercise, take ten minutes and write 2 or 3 paragraphs of your understanding of how your money history resulted in you having the Money Blueprint that now rules your life.

If you've applied yourself in these exercises, you will be able to identify a correlation between your Money Profiles in your Money Blueprint and where they originated from in your past money history.

Often when people make this link, they suddenly heave a sigh of relief. They realise and understand where their Money Blueprint comes from and see the reason for them having the Blueprint they have.

People often feel hugely energised at this stage to start taking steps to modify something they have lived with all their lives.

Summary:

Strength in Money Types 1, 2 and 4 indicate some distance between you and the money world. This sometimes plays out in you never allowing yourself to get close to money and will often result in people with this Money Profile never making huge amounts of money.

What is important to realise here, is that it doesn't mean you can't be successful. In fact, now for the first time ever, you have your best chance at success.

Because you have never had a close relationship with money before doesn't mean you can't start building that relationship now. In fact, it's a relatively easy job. Once you have taken your Money Profile and understood from whence it came, by reviewing it in conjunction with your Money Biography, you will have a good idea of the source of your money beliefs.

These beliefs were what you understood at the time they were established, probably when you were young. They were beliefs that made good sense when you were young, but let's face it – they no longer serve you.

So, you have a choice. You can continue for the rest of your days, carrying this burden of an old belief system that doesn't serve you, or you can take the first step towards change. If this is your choice (and it might not be), then your first step is towards building up your confidence and understanding of the money world and Real Estate. This will take time! This will take energy! But it will also deliver results.

If you began to read some of the Rich-Dad-Poor-Dad books. If you began listening and reading financial TV and Radio programs, reading books on Real Estate, and playing financial board games, particularly Rich Dads Cashflow Quadrants for 6 months, you'd be amazed at the changes you will feel.

Your fear will dissipate. You will feel more confident and competent in your dealings on money matters. You will feel what some people with this Money Profile describe as fuzziness, lack of clarity, fear or avoidance of money related issues disappear. You will slowly feel better equipped to make financial decisions and take financial action.

If your Money Profile shows evidence of a strong number 3, you will feel confident and well able to analyse the investment opportunity before you. You will feel able to focus and understand the pros and cons, you will feel able to run the numbers and formulate a set of options to consider. You will be able to balance the risk v reward attributes. This Money Profile gives you the best chance of succeeding in pretty much any financial opportunity whether it be a conventional business, a property or Crypto opportunity.

You will use your skill to evaluate the opportunity, you will timeously make a decision and mostly, unless there are issues that still require exploring, you will act immediately and produce results.

Lastly, but my no means least, dominance in Money Type 5 needs the proverbial "Hand brake". People with a dominance in Money Profile 5 can be hugely successful but beware, the devil is in the detail. You will see an opportunity and before doing any proper analysis, before doing a risk analysis or even running any numbers, you'll dive in. You'll invest large amounts of money in high risk, high return opportunities.

This can be great, because many times the pendulum will swing to your side and you'll make a killing. However, equally possible is that the opportunity turns upside down and you lose your investment. If you're strong in this Money Profile and you are unfortunate and make a loss, you are unlikely to learn from your mistake. The chances are that you will get up after being knocked down, brush yourself off and get ready for the next financial opportunity.

You have a delightfully positive optimism about everything but you are likely to waste a lot of time, energy and money because of your light-hearted approach to money.

Conclusion:

Generally, your single best approach to any Real Estate investment is to pull up the Hand Brake and stop. Don't act! Wait! Read! Analyse. Run the numbers. Work out the breakeven point, understand what you're doing, do your costings and understand the buoyancy or otherwise of the market sector you are interested in.

In short, go home and sleep on it. Do your research and slowly allow your decision to evolve.

Investing in Real Estate is sometime scary, sometimes exciting. Both huge profits and extreme losses can be made. It is strongly advised that if you feel that this asset class is what you'd like to invest in, you should make certain that you do your homework and most important, you MUST LEARN to run the numbers.

Lastly, If you've done the excercises in this short eBook you will have an understanding of your Money History and your Money Blueprint. Well done. This insight will stand you in good stead for all your future investement and business decisions. Make your decisions keeping what you have learnt from this book in the forfront of your mind and you will increase you success rate exponentially.

Above all - share your love with someone you care about right now. Its a great way to begin any journey.

www.ingramcontent.com/pod-product-compliance
Lightning Source LLC
Chambersburg PA
CBHW031512210526
45463CB00008B/3211